Would You Rather...?

Youth Specialties resources written by Doug Fields

Creative Bible Lessons on the Life of Christ
Help! I'm a Volunteer Youth Worker
Purpose-Driven™ Youth Ministry
Purpose-Driven™ Youth Ministry Training Kit
Screen Play

Youth Specialties books coauthored by Doug Fields

Memory Makers
(with Duffy Robbins)

Spontaneous Melodramas
(with Laurie Polich & Duffy Robbins)

Spontaneous Melodramas 2
(with Laurie Polich & Duffy Robbins)

Videos That Teach
(with Eddie James)

Videos That Teach 2
(with Eddie James)

Check us out at *www.YouthSpecialties.com*!

Would You Rather...?

465 Provocative Questions
to Get Teenagers Talking

Doug Fields

GRAND RAPIDS, MICHIGAN 49530 USA

Would You Rather ...? 465 Provocative Questions to Get Teenagers Talking

Copyright © 1995 Youth Specialties

Youth Specialties Books, 300 S. Pierce St., El Cajon, CA 92020 are published by Zondervan Publishing House, 5300 Patterson Ave. SE, Grand Rapids, MI 49530.

Edited by Noel Becchetti
Cover design by Proxy
Interior design by Youth Specialties

Printed in the United States of America

01 02 03 04 05 06 07 / CH / 17 16 15 14 13 12 11

Contents

To Greg & Linda Vujnov
Great friends, great youth workers, and
the King & Queen of *Would You Rather ...?*

Thanks also to some friends who added
some of their ideas to this book: Heidi Brown,
Nancy Davis, Cathy Fields, Jason France,
Phillip Hamer, Dan Hamer, Cynthia Hammork,
Tic Long, Jasmine Mohiuddin, Ken
Robertson, and Sabrina Scherf.

The History of *Would You Rather ...?*

One warm summer night, I was sitting with 12 students on a houseboat where there was no music, television, or phone. From 8:00 p.m. until 2:00 a.m. we shared the beautiful gift of conversation. It was a night I'll never forget. All the talking started with the simple question, "Would you rather drink Coke or Pepsi?" As I watched these normally apathetic students passionately argue their position and try to persuade their peers to their brand of soft drink, I remember thinking, "I wish these students would become this passionate about their faith."

Then I followed up with the question, "Would you rather be rich or famous?" We were off! We talked, argued, laughed, disagreed, and discovered the decision-making process and values of each student. For the remainder of the houseboat trip, the students kept asking "would you rather" questions. These questions were funny, stupid, serious, and intriguing.

In this book you will find dozens of questions to help get your students talking. You'll discover your favorites as well as come up with some of your own. Mark your favorites in this book so you can quickly flip to them. My experience is that these *Would You Rather ...?* questions are like good jokes—they're tough to remember.

Have fun talking!

Doug Fields

How to Use *Would You Rather ...?*

My goals in asking students these questions are to:
1. Get students talking;
2. Discover their decision-making process; and
3. Challenge and encourage their responses.

Keeping some basic concepts in mind will help you better use these questions.

Use the Right Question at the Right Time

Some of the *Would You Rather ...?* questions have no significant value. They will receive quick answers requiring little to no thought, such as #101 (...get caught picking your nose or pulling your underwear out?). This type of question is intended to warm up your group and doesn't necessarily need much follow-up discussion.

Other questions require more serious, in-depth responses—such as #247 (...have no values or no friends?). Save these questions for times when you want to draw kids out on their deep-seated opinions and beliefs.

Create Your Own Rules

Some of the questions will require you to

provide additional information and/or boundaries. For example:

> **Leader:** "Would you rather be rich or famous?"
> **Student:** "That's easy. Famous—because if I were famous I'd automatically be rich."
> **Leader:** "Okay, let me rephrase the question. Would you rather be rich without ever having any fame or famous without ever being rich?"

When you provide additional elements to the question, you force the student to do more thinking that will give you some indication of his or her values. I might follow up with a question about a student's desire to be wealthy. In this answer he or she is most likely to enlighten me about his or her value-system.

Push a Little

Some of your students will answer "neither" to your *Would You Rather ...?* questions, such as #302 (...dress like your parents or act like them?). The "neither" answer is an easy out. Challenge your students to give you an answer anyway. Usually, any type of answer can lead to more discussion or provide some insight into their thinking.

Be Sensitive

Be wise when deciding which questions to ask. If I have a student with a bad case of acne, I wouldn't ask #94 (...have terrible acne or be bald?) Questions having to do with appearance need to be thought through for the potential impact on a given student.

Code Your Favorites

As you read through the book, create codes for your favorite questions. For example, I put an *F* next to the questions that I think are *funny* and know will get a laugh. I write *DD* next to the questions that I know will cause us to *dig deeper* in our conversation. A *hot topic* that will create some heated debate gets an *HT*. This type of coding helps me quickly flip to my favorites.

Would You Rather...?

1

...be rich or famous?

2

...die by fire or by drowning?

3

...have your friends think that you're stuck on yourself or that you're a wimp?

4

...steal from an old lady or laugh out loud at a funeral?

5

…drink Coke or Pepsi?

6

…be male or female?

7

…go on a camping vacation or vacation at a resort?

8

…sweat because of exercise or because of humidity?

9

...watch television or read a book?

10

...be the President of the United States or the world's richest person?

11

...ride a roller coaster or a mechanical bull?

12

...be told you have a booger hanging from your nose or told you have bad breath?

13

...have the power to fly or the
power to disappear?

14

...step in dog poop barefoot or have
a bird-dropping hit you
on the head?

15

...dress casually or fancy?

16

...have blistered lips or paper cuts
on each finger?

17

...have diarrhea or be constipated?

18

...be caught cutting classes or have almost everyone believe wrongly that you were drunk at a school event?

19

...be thrown off a horse or body-slammed by a wrestler?

20

...give up your favorite food forever or television for two years?

21

...be healthy and homeless or
have the AIDS virus and live in luxury?

22

...fail in business and end up bankrupt or fail
in marriage and end up divorced?

23

...live in Los Angeles or in
New York City?

24

...eat Mexican food or Chinese food?

25
...be bald or have no toes?

26
...have a small tattoo on your neck or wear jewelry through your nose?

27
...have one romantic date with someone you're attracted to or briefly meet your hero?

28
...hang wallpaper or scrub floors?

29

…be addicted to drugs or alcohol?

30

…eat too little and be hungry or
too much and be sick?

31

…be ugly and have 10 good friends or
attractive and have only one good friend?

32

…die without warning or
die slowly, surrounded by family and friends?

33
...be bitten by a shark or
by a pit bull dog?

34
...be a famous athlete or
a famous rock musician?

35
...be obese or emaciated?

36
...have straight hair or curly hair?

37

...be known as a bad kisser or
someone with bad breath?

38

...be embarrassed in front of friends
or in front of strangers?

39

...receive daily encouragement from your
boss or a five percent pay raise?

40

...buy an American car or
a foreign car?

41

...be woken up by music or
by an alarm?

42

...travel with the circus or
a minor-league baseball team?

43

...be a movie star or a television star?

44

...live in the city or in the country?

45

…travel by train or by plane?

46

…walk on hot sand while barefoot or
have sand thrown in your face?

47

…be kicked in the groin or
hit in the mouth?

48

…have your leg amputated or
your arm amputated?

49

...be grossed-out or frightened?

50

...fall off your bicycle or
run into a tree while jogging?

51

...roller skate or ice skate?

52

...drive a $30,000 car you don't own or
keep the interest from the $30,000?

53

…listen to a news station or
a music station?

54

…eat pie or ice cream?

55

…be a baby again or a 50-year-old?

56

…pay for a $100 traffic ticket or
lose $100?

57
...use an Apple computer or an IBM?

58
...drive a Ford or a Chevy?

59
...be hot or cold?

60
...wake up early or sleep in late?

61

…drink from a bottle or from a can?

62

…wear Nikes or Reeboks?

63

…be considered rich and live in Haiti or poor and live in the United States?

64

…own a dog or a cat?

65

…watch a drama or a comedy?

66

…be Michael Jordan or Mother Teresa?

67

…have labor pains or dry heaves?

68

…explore under the sea or outer space?

69
...be sick at home for a week or in the hospital for two days?

70
...swim in the ocean or in a pool?

71
...eat a burrito or a piece of pizza?

72
...be 7' 6" tall or 4' 2"?

73
...go to an opera or a county fair?

74
...talk to your best friend who lives
2,000 miles away from home
over the phone for one hour or
see this friend in person for five minutes?

75
...eat yogurt or ice cream?

76
...water ski or snow ski?

77

...own a cabin in the mountains or
a home on the beach?

78

...lie to your friend or have
your friend lie to you?

79

...scrape your knee or pick off a scab?

80

...eat ice cream from a cone or from a cup?

81

...go blind or deaf?

82

...get poked in the eye with a sharp stick or have your hand nibbled on by a cannibal?

83

...be known for your looks or
for your personality?

84

...shop for clothes during a crowded sale or
pay regular price with personal service?

85

...see an R-rated movie or a G-rated one?

86

...have a big rear or a big nose?

87

...be trapped in an elevator or
caught in bumper-to-bumper traffic?

88

...die of cancer or of AIDS?

89
…have the chills or a fever?

90
…eat chocolate ice cream or vanilla?

91
…have sextuplets (6) or be infertile?

92
…be a doctor or a lawyer?

93

...be verbally abused or slapped in the face?

94

...have terrible acne or be bald?

95

...go to Disneyland or visit a friend you haven't seen in five years?

96

...have a housekeeper or a chauffeur?

97
…be blonde or brunette?

98
…be a student or an employee?

99
…wln $10,000 or earn $1,000,000?

100
…take a nap in a hammock or on the beach?

101

…get caught picking your nose or pulling your underwear out?

102

…read the book or see the movie?

103

…be known for your intelligence or your personality?

104

…eat liver or sushi?

105
...have excessive nose hair or
excessive ear hair?

106
...find someone's hair on your plate or see a
cockroach on your food?

107
...be gossiped about or lied to?

108
...take risks with your money or
make safe investments?

109

…tell the host the food is terrible and not eat it or eat the food and pretend to like it?

110

…be in jail and allowed visitors or deserted on an island in total isolation?

111

…watch a sunset or a sunrise?

112

…browse through a bookstore or a record store?

113

…watch a soap opera or make fun of one?

114

…talk to everyone at a crowded party for a short time or have a significant conversation with two people?

115

…be spanked or put on restriction?

116

…have more money than time or more time than money?

117

...eat a bad meal in a restaurant or
a good meal in your home?

118

...be remembered as a good parent or
a good child?

119

...be an artist or a musician?

120

...be highly educated or highly successful?

121

...go to war or be a conscientious objector?

122

...be friends with Muhammad Ali or
Hank Aaron?

123

...read fiction or nonfiction?

124

...laugh really hard one day a week or
laugh a little every day?

125
…make a child cry or kick a puppy?

126
…watch one hundred hours of Sesame Street or a boring documentary?

127
…look stupid or be stupid?

128
…walk on the moon or be President of the United States for a week?

129

...hit the winning home run in a World Series game or score a touchdown in the Super Bowl?

130

...watch a situation comedy or a made-for-TV movie?

131

...write a best seller or be a cover model for a national magazine?

132

...faint during your wedding ceremony and recover an hour later or throw up during your ceremony and continue right away?

133

...crash your parents' car or
your sibling's car?

134

...be known as a generous giver or
someone who is full of joy?

135

...sky dive or hang glide?

136

...crack your head open or
have minor hemorrhoid surgery?

137
...ruin your favorite shirt or
spill coffee on a stranger's outfit?

138
...eat a bar of soap or
drink a bottle of dishwasher liquid?

139
...get hit by a car going 60 miles
an hour and live, or fall from a
10-story building and live?

140
...drink coffee in the middle of a scorching
desert or drink a Slurpee in the middle of a
snow storm?

141

...purchase a car without any assistance or buy one from a knowledgeable but pushy salesperson?

142

...eat a shark sandwich after scuba diving or eat a hamburger after branding a wild steer?

143

...eat a cookie or cookie dough?

144

...have a stupid-looking haircut or a fat lip?

145

...give money to a religious cult or to an abortion clinic?

146

...go hiking or watch television?

147

...be inside the house on a sunny day or outside on a rainy day?

148

...eat a hamburger in front of a starving child or destroy a child's self-image?

149
...clean out a garage
or assemble a swing set?

150
...give a speech in front of 10,000 people or
be arrested while on national television?

151
...smuggle cocaine into the U.S. or
Mexican citizens across the border?

152
...have a life full of good memories or a life
full of exciting adventures you couldn't
remember?

153
...be known as someone who is arrogant or someone who is untrustworthy?

154
...be a half hour early to a party or an hour-and-a-half late?

155
...lose all of your photo albums or all of your savings account?

156
...have a stomachache or a headache?

157

…eat only chicken or only red meat?

158

…eat thick crust pizza or thin crust pizza?

159

…watch professional football or college football?

160

…get shot from a cannon or walk the high wire?

161

...go swimming or shopping?

162

...drink diet or regular soft drinks?

163

...know the sex of your unborn child or be surprised?

164

...cheat on a test and receive an A or not cheat and get a D?

165

...be captured by a ghost or by an alien?

166

...wear really tight pants or really loose pants?

167

...die lonely with no enemies or die hated by many?

168

...get a shot from a doctor or get a filling by the dentist?

169

...die before your spouse or
have your spouse die before you?

170

...be a famous national hero or discover a
cure for cancer and receive no recognition?

171

...swim like a fish or fly like a bird?

172

...be a police officer or a firefighter?

173
...have a great body or a great mind?

174
...know you only have one year to live or
die unexpectedly?

175
...betray your spouse or
be betrayed by your spouse?

176
...eat squid or chocolate-covered ants?

177

…run a 26-mile marathon or
swim five miles?

178

…get a flat tire or run out of gas?

179

…go to jail for life without the possibility of
parole or die in the gas chamber?

180

…read 500 pages from the Bible or
100 pages about medieval politics?

181

…have a runny nose or itchy eyes?

182

…have your date tell you that you have really bad breath or endure your date's horrid breath?

183

…eat a candy bar or a piece of fruit?

184

…be thirsty or have a full bladder and not be able to relieve yourself for an hour?

185
…wear uncomfortable shoes or
a hat that's too tight?

186
…confront someone about lying or
let it slide and try to forget about it?

187
…pick out your wedding ring or
be surprised by your fiancé?

188
…be booed by 50,000 fans watching you play
a sport or be booed at your high school
reunion?

189

...play a sport or be a spectator?

190

...be yelled at by a friend or by a stranger?

191

...be afraid of the dark or be claustrophobic?

192

...have compulsive behaviors or be apathetic?

193

...spend your life in a wheelchair or on crutches?

194

...be anorexic and starve yourself or be bulimic and throw your food up?

195

...be a liberal or a fundamentalist?

196

...read *Newsweek* or *Sports Illustrated*?

197
...be a doctor for the terminally ill or be terminally ill?

198
...live with the *Bonanza* family or the *Munster* family?

199
...work for the FBI or for NASA?

200
...have your head chopped off by a guillotine or face a firing squad?

201

...live in the U.S. during the Great Depression or in present-day Haiti?

202

...be trampled by humans during a riot or kicked around by a rodeo bull?

203

...vacation in Tahiti or in the French Alps?

204

...be known as a racist or as a traitor to your country?

205

...live on an ocean vessel for a year or on a space station for the same amount of time?

206

...freeze to death or burn to death?

207

...be Martin Luther King or Mohandas "Mahatma" Gandhi?

208

...discover gold or oil?

209

…watch a best friend die in an accident or
20 people die who you don't know?

210

…own a McDonald's franchise in a
busy location or have $100,000?

211

…be married to someone who can't speak or
to someone who can't see?

212

…drive a tank during a war or
work on an aircraft carrier?

213

…lie to your mom or to your spouse?

214

…go a week without brushing your teeth or without taking a shower?

215

…win a spelling bee or a speech contest?

216

…dive into a pool of acid or swim in a pond full of blood-sucking leeches?

217
...live in pain for the rest of your life or
die within a week?

218
...have a messy bedroom or
dirty kitchen floors?

219
...have 12 children or none?

220
...be a famous basketball star and die at 42
or live to be 90 without any fame?

221

...put together a 300,000-piece jigsaw puzzle or read the dictionary from cover to cover?

222

...eat your favorite food every day for the rest of your life or a variety of foods you hate?

223

...be lost in a jungle or in a desert?

224

...be forced to watch five hours of TV news every day or give up TV forever?

225

...do something you hate and make $100,000 a year or something you enjoy and make $20,000 a year?

226

...be a teenager in the 1950s or today?

227

...meet Leonardo da Vinci or Benjamin Franklin?

228

...be an only child or one of 10 children?

229

…wear dirty underwear or dirty socks?

230

…be cremated or buried?

231

…be on the cover of *Time* magazine or on the cover of *People* magazine?

232

…see Elvis return from the dead or John Lennon return from the dead?

233

...meet Fred Flintstone or Yogi Bear?

234

...work at a job that was challenging or one that was easy?

235

...be extremely shy or have a guilty conscience?

236

...drive a BMW and make $10,000 a year or drive a scooter and make $100,000 a year?

237

...lose both of your index fingers or six of your toes?

238

...be told you remind people of Jeffrey Dahmer or of Adolf Hitler?

239

...drive a fancy car for 20,000 miles or a beat-up car for 100,000 miles?

240

...receive a lump sum of $168,000 or $14,000 a month for a year?

241

...drop a 15-pound bowling ball on your foot
or get your finger slammed in a car door?

242

...have your best friend steal your
favorite piece of jewelry and then have to
confront the situation, or have the jewelry
mysteriously disappear?

243

...have a huge house with no furniture or a
tiny house with a lot of furniture?

244

...admit to a fear or
do something you don't want to do?

245

...be nearsighted or farsighted?

246

...be fluent in seven languages and never leave the United States or travel the world by yourself and be unable to speak with anyone?

247

...have no values or no friends?

248

...have all your fingers broken or one of your legs broken?

249

...be made fun of by a few or
ignored by many?

250

...see your best friend go to jail for 10 years
or go to jail yourself for two years?

251

...jam your finger in a basketball game or
stub your toe on a brick?

252

...be a turtle or a snail?

253
...get sat on by an elephant or swallowed by a whale?

254
...be a cartoonist or a sports columnist?

255
...meet William Shakespeare or Andrew Lloyd Webber?

256
...step in Jell-O or mashed potatoes?

257

...have one good friend for life or lots of friends for a short time?

258

...be unable to use your arms or unable to use your legs?

259

...hit your knee on a table or your elbow on a corner?

260

...have your room painted purple or neon yellow?

261

...be a drunk driver who kills someone or
a husband whose wife is killed
by a drunk driver?

262

...be a soccer ball or a football?

263

...have a strawberry seed or
a popcorn kernel stuck between your teeth?

264

...eat liver or Spam?

265
...design toilet seat covers or install them?

266
...meet Hillary or Roseanne?

267
...be in 120° weather or -20° weather?

268
...be cute and stupid or smart and ugly?

269

...be in the Olympics for one event and never play sports again or play on a minor-league team for 15 years?

270

...get four billion dollars and be exiled from your homeland or stay where you are now with all your friends and have no money?

271

...lose your spouse or your child?

272

...eat a night crawler or a cockroach?

273

...swim through smelly sewer water or walk across hot coals with your bare feet?

274

...weigh 75 pounds or 350 pounds?

275

...marry a rich, beautiful person who is mean or a poor, ugly person who is nice?

276

...have a large birthmark that covers your face or never be able to talk to anyone?

277

…be a musician or a poet?

278

…be a proud grandparent or
discover the Fountain of Youth?

279

…read a book or listen to music?

280

…know all there is to know in the universe or
experience love?

281
...finger paint with a class of first graders or do graffiti with gang members?

282
...burp out loud or pass gas silently?

283
...believe you are right, stand your ground, and have someone say "I hate you," or compromise?

284
...break a promise or break a heart?

285

…watch Joe Montana throw an 80-yard
Super Bowl-winning touchdown pass or
play catch with your dad?

286

…live a life of luxury or
be known for your generosity?

287

…have a phone that dials directly to the
President of the United States or speak to the
Creator of the Universe from your own heart?

288

…give or receive?

289

…figure out the solution to a problem or let someone who has already been through it advise you?

290

…be the person who vomits or the person who has to clean up the vomit?

291

…decide if and when to pull the plug on your comatose parents or have them die unexpectedly?

292

…walk one mile or run ten 100-yard sprints?

293
...be a girl with a mustache or
a guy with a high soprano voice?

294
...die a slow painful death or
die instantly in a car crash?

295
...have the career of Amy Grant or
the heart of Mother Teresa?

296
...have insomnia for one month or
night terrors for one month?

297
...have a fly in your soup or
a slug in your salad?

298
...own an expensive piece of diamond
jewelry and never be able to wear it or
wear a nice-looking Cubic Zirconium?

299
...have a pimple on the tip of your nose or
a blister on your heel?

300
...walk on hot coals or lay on a bed of nails?

301

...make a difference in the world and be unknown or be famous for doing nothing?

302

...dress like your parents or act like them?

303

...pierce your bellybutton or your eyebrow?

304

...have your thumb accidentally cut off or your forefinger accidentally cut off?

305

...eat dog food or cat food?

306

...be average looking and sighted or the most gorgeous person in the world but blind?

307

...have one thick bushy eyebrow or long nose hairs?

308

...be a person who survived World War II in a Nazi concentration camp or a guard in the same camp who had to perform executions?

309

...have huge ears or be hard of hearing?

310

...have a disabled baby or no children at all?

311

...be locked out of your car or your house?

312

...work in a psychiatric ward for a year with no pay or be admitted to the ward for six months?

313

...move to a place where people are starving or a place where the diet consists of monkey brains and maggots?

314

...have hot itchy feet or hot itchy armpits?

315

...repay your debts or file for bankruptcy?

316

...be awakened at 2:00 a.m. by a phone call or by a knock on your door?

317
...be the parent of a rebellious teenager or
the parent of a deaf child?

318
...meet Jesus for four hours or
travel with the Apostle Paul for three years?

319
...fly a kite or play jump rope?

320
...watch a game on TV or
see the game in person?

321

…vacation in a five-star, first-class resort in South Dakota or in a tent in Hawaii?

322

…have X-ray vision or the ability to read minds?

323

…have a tail like a monkey or whiskers like a kitten?

324

…sleep on flannel sheets or satin sheets?

325

…be on the *David Letterman Show* or the *Today* show?

326

…read a road map while driving or stop and ask for directions?

327

…pull weeds or prune trees?

328

…be a street sweeper at Disneyland or an assistant manager at Taco Bell?

329

...use 2-ply or 1-ply toilet paper?

330

...meet Carol Burnett or Lucille Ball?

331

...have a canker sore on your mouth or a sty in your eye?

332

...memorize the chart of chemical elements or be able to identify 50 constellations?

333

...watch *Barney* or *Sesame Street*?

334

...hitchhike across the USA or
sneak rides on freight trains across the USA?

335

...sneeze for an hour or hiccup for an hour?

336

...live in Oz or Narnia?

337

...have a roommate who snores or one who talks in his or her sleep?

338

...have a flat tire in the fast lane of the freeway or run out of gas in the middle of the desert?

339

...be stung by one bee or by 10 red ants?

340

...be kept awake by a barking dog or by wind chimes?

341

...have broccoli stuck in your teeth or something hanging out of your nose?

342

...know that your spouse had a one-night stand or never find out?

343

...have three eyeballs or webbed feet?

344

...teach a Bible study or attend a Bible study?

345

...own your own dream house that is furnished with thrift-shop furniture or rent a small apartment that is fully furnished with specialty-store furniture?

346

...be able to fly or to run faster than sound?

347

...walk under a ladder or step on a crack?

348

...wear someone else's dirty socks or someone else's dirty shirt?

349
...watch your favorite movie of all time seven times in a row or a really horrible movie only once?

350
...bite your tongue or burn your tongue?

351
...live with the Brady Bunch or with the Partridge Family?

352
...have an appointment with a proctologist or an appointment with a psychoanalyst?

353

...go on a computer date set up by your mother or a blind date set up by her?

354

...eat pâté or caviar?

355

...be liked by others or
be happy without friends?

356

...overpay your taxes and not get a refund or
cheat on your taxes and get a huge refund?

357

…live a long boring life or
live hard and die young?

358

…be short and proud or tall and shy?

359

…be rich and alone or
poor with lots of friends?

360

…wear a suit with sneakers or
short pants with colored dress socks?

361

...be abducted by aliens or put in jail?

362

...fall in love and lose that person or never fall in love at all?

363

...be a farmer or a politician?

364

...travel the stars or live under the sea?

365
...live in fear or die in bravery?

366
...try everything and succeed at nothing or try only one thing and succeed?

367
...paint for 10 hours or swim for 10 hours?

368
...live a lie or lie to live?

369

...lose a leg or lose a loved one?

370

...lose your mind or lose your soul?

371

...go blind or deaf?

372

...get a perm or have your head shaved?

373

...stay in one spot all your life or
travel the world and never settle down?

374

...go bald or have your hair turn gray?

375

...drive all your life and get in weekly
accidents or never drive?

376

...be a teacher or a learner?

377
...give your time or your money?

378
...talk with the President of the
United States or with Billy Graham?

379
...love your friends or
have your friends love you?

380
...help or be helped?

381

...laugh or make others laugh?

382

...lead one close friend to Christ through your example or lead 20 strangers to Christ through your preaching?

383

...take communion or sing worship songs?

384

...take care of the very old or the very young?

385

...stay in one place and have lots of friends
or travel and have few friends?

386

...work hard to gain what you want or
have it given to you?

387

...grow your own garden or
have flowers given to you?

388

...take care of animals or people?

389
...be able to eat what you want without gaining weight or have a wonderful talent?

390
...avoid challenge or seek it out?

391
...cover up your troubles or let them out and try to work on them?

392
...climb a mountain or read a good novel?

393
...play more or accomplish more?

394
...spend time with your family or
with your friends?

395
...take a bath or a shower?

396
...be a great influence or
be greatly influenced?

397

…forgive or be forgiven?

398

…be a good athlete or a good scholar?

399

…go to church every day for two months or
skip youth group for six months?

400

…watch *Baywatch* alone or
with someone to make fun of the acting?

401

...find your dad reading *Playboy* or a Barney coloring book?

402

...give money to a friend or to a stranger?

403

...embarrass yourself or have your parents embarrass you?

404

...eat spinach or liver?

405

...eat sauerkraut or liverwurst?

406

...forget to take your wallet to the mall or your homework to school?

407

...be asked out by someone you don't like or be turned down by someone you do?

408

...be the worst player on a championship team or the best player on a last place team?

409

...wear underwear that is too tight or underwear that is filled with holes?

410

...get low scores on your SAT test or fail your driver's test?

411

...be hungry or thirsty?

412

...live without TV or without music?

413

…meet the President or Madonna?

414

…be the oldest child in the family or the youngest?

415

…drive an expensive sports car or be chauffeured in a limo?

416

…be the only Christian at a wild party or the only non-Christian at a Bible study?

417

...deliver babies or pizzas?

418

...give your testimony in front of friends or in front of strangers?

419

...attend a parent-teacher conference with your mom or with your dad?

420

...win the Heisman Trophy or the Nobel Peace Prize?

421
...watch *Star Trek* or *Gilligan's Island*?

422
...attend the Last Supper or discover Jesus' empty tomb?

423
...have lunch with Judas or with John the Baptist?

424
...be Captain Kirk or Captain Kangaroo?

425
...be the President of Haiti or
the President of General Motors?

426
...read a good book or watch a good movie?

427
...be a photographer for *Sports Illustrated* or
for *Victoria's Secret*?

428
...be trapped in an elevator with Barney or
with Forrest Gump?

429

...pass out Christian literature at an airport or work at a greasy hot dog stand?

430

...be wanted or needed?

431

...discover a cure for cancer or a cure for AIDS?

432

...be a teacher or a student?

433

...be run over by a car and unable to walk again or be the driver to run over and kill a stranger?

434

...have athlete's foot or dandruff?

435

...be misunderstood or misinformed?

436

...win by cheating or lose while playing fair?

437

...work outdoors with your hands or indoors at a desk job?

438

...get caught cheating or lying?

439

...be funny or kind?

440

...be homeless or friendless?

441

…have a high-paying job and travel 50 percent of the time or an average-paying job with no travel?

442

…be born blind with a 50 percent chance of gaining sight or go blind forever at age 10?

443

…be poor or stupid?

444

…have good grades and a bad reputation or bad grades and a good reputation?

445
…be the Pope or
the President of the United States?

446
…be Abraham Lincoln or George
Washington?

447
…be a librarian or a chemist?

448
…be covered with Cheez Whiz or sour
cream?

449
...feel guilty or be guilty?

450
...be covered with spiders or with snakes?

451
...hear someone snap their gum or crack their knuckles?

452
...scratch a chalkboard or bite down on tin-foil?

453
...have intestinal worms or head lice?

454
...have acne on your face or
warts all over your hands?

455
...have a migraine headache or bad gas
pains?

456
...have a runny nose or a stuffed nose?

457

...sell used cars or Amway?

458

...have a life filled with sadness but help others or have a happy, carefree life and make no difference in the world?

459

...be double-crossed by a friend or beat up by a stranger?

460

...wear a hairpiece or dentures?

461

...have a wedgie or wet armpits?

462

...walk three miles to school every day or be dropped off at school in front of your friends in an old, beat-up clunker?

463

...have college paid for but not get a choice of where you go, or go anywhere you want but pay for your entire college education?

464

...be convicted of something you didn't do or see someone else convicted for something you did?

465

…keep answering these questions or send the author some questions for his next *Would You Rather …?* book?

Send them to:
Doug Fields
c/o Making Young Lives Count
21612 Plano Trabuco, #Q-30
Trabuco Canyon, CA 92679
e-mail: Linda@dougfields.com
www.youthministryonline.com

Resources from Youth Specialties

Ideas Library
Ideas Library on CD-ROM 2.0
Administration, Publicity, & Fundraising
Camps, Retreats, Missions, & Service Ideas
Creative Meetings, Bible Lessons, & Worship Ideas
Crowd Breakers & Mixers
Discussion & Lesson Starters
Discussion & Lesson Starters 2
Drama, Skits, & Sketches
Drama, Skits, & Sketches 2
Drama, Skits, & Sketches 3
Games
Games 2
Games 3
Holiday Ideas
Special Events

Bible Curricula
Creative Bible Lessons from the Old Testament
Creative Bible Lessons in 1 & 2 Corinthians
Creative Bible Lessons in Galatians and Philippians
Creative Bible Lessons in John
Creative Bible Lessons in Romans
Creative Bible Lessons on the Life of Christ
Creative Bible Lessons in Psalms
Downloading the Bible Kit
Wild Truth Bible Lessons
Wild Truth Bible Lessons 2
Wild Truth Bible Lessons—Pictures of God
Wild Truth Bible Lessons—Pictures of God 2

Topical Curricula
Creative Junior High Programs from A to Z, Vol. 1 (A-M)
Creative Junior High Programs from A to Z, Vol. 2 (N-Z)
Girls: 10 Gutsy, God-Centered Sessions on Issues That Matter to Girls
Guys: 10 Fearless, Faith-Focused Sessions on Issues That Matter to Guys
Good Sex
Live the Life! Student Evangelism Training Kit
The Next Level Youth Leader's Kit
Roaring Lambs
So What Am I Gonna Do with My Life?
Student Leadership Training Manual
Student Underground
Talking the Walk
What Would Jesus Do? Youth Leader's Kit
Wild Truth Bible Lessons
Wild Truth Bible Lessons 2
Wild Truth Bible Lessons—Pictures of God

Discussion Starters
Discussion & Lesson Starters (Ideas Library)
Discussion & Lesson Starters 2 (Ideas Library)
EdgeTV
Every Picture Tells a Story
Get 'Em Talking
Keep 'Em Talking!
High School TalkSheets—Updated!
More High School TalkSheets—Updated!
High School TalkSheets from Psalms and Proverbs—Updated!
Junior High-Middle School TalkSheets—Updated!

More Junior High-Middle School TalkSheets—Updated!
Junior High-Middle School TalkSheets from Psalms and Proverbs—Updated!
Small Group Qs
Have You Ever...?
Unfinished Sentences
What If...?
Would You Rather...?

Drama Resources
Drama, Skits, & Sketches (Ideas Library)
Drama, Skits, & Sketches 2 (Ideas Library)
Drama, Skits, & Sketches 3 (Ideas Library)
Dramatic Pauses
Spontaneous Melodramas
Spontaneous Melodramas 2
Super Sketches for Youth Ministry

Game Resources
Games (Ideas Library)
Games 2 (Ideas Library)
Games 3 (Ideas Library)
Junior High Game Nights
More Junior High Game Nights
Play It!
Screen Play CD-ROM

Additional Programming
(also see Discussion Starters)
Camps, Retreats, Missions, & Service Ideas (Ideas Library)
Creative Meetings, Bible Lessons, & Worship Ideas (Ideas Library)
Crowd Breakers & Mixers (Ideas Library)
Everyday Object Lessons
Great Fundraising Ideas for Youth Groups
More Great Fundraising Ideas for Youth Groups
Great Retreats for Youth Groups
Great Talk Outlines for Youth Ministry
Holiday Ideas (Ideas Library)
Incredible Questionnaires for Youth Ministry
Kickstarters
Memory Makers
Special Events (Ideas Library)
Videos That Teach
Videos That Teach 2
Worship Services for Youth Groups

Quick Question Books
Have You Ever...?
Small Group Qs
Unfinished Sentences
What If...?
Would You Rather...?

Videos & Video Curricula
Dynamic Communicators Workshop
EdgeTV
Live the Life! Student Evangelism Training Kit
Make 'Em Laugh!
Purpose-DrivenTM Youth Ministry Training Kit
Student Underground
Understanding Your Teenager Video Curriculum
Youth Ministry outside the Lines

Especially for Junior High
Creative Junior High Programs from A to Z, Vol. 1 (A-M)
Creative Junior High Programs from A to Z, Vol. 2 (N-Z)
Junior High Game Nights
More Junior High Game Nights
Junior High-Middle School TalkSheets—Updated!

More Junior High-Middle School TalkSheets—Updated!
Junior High-Middle School TalkSheets from Psalms and Proverbs—Updated!
Wild Truth Journal for Junior Highers
Wild Truth Bible Lessons
Wild Truth Bible Lessons 2
Wild Truth Journal—Pictures of God
Wild Truth Bible Lessons—Pictures of God
Wild Truth Bible Lessons—Pictures of God 2

Student Resources
Downloading the Bible: A Rough Guide to the New Testament
Downloading the Bible: A Rough Guide to the Old Testament
Grow for It! Journal through the Scriptures
So What Am I Gonna Do with My Life?
Spiritual Challenge Journal: The Next Level
Teen Devotional Bible
What (Almost) Nobody Will Tell You about Sex
What Would Jesus Do? Spiritual Challenge Journal

Clip Art
Youth Group Activities (print)
Clip Art Library Version 2.0 (CD-ROM)

Digital Resources
Clip Art Library Version 2.0 (CD-ROM)
Great Talk Outlines for Youth Ministry
Hot Illustrations CD-ROM
Ideas Library on CD-ROM 2.0
Screen Play
Youth Ministry Management Tools

Professional Resources
Administration, Publicity, & Fundraising (Ideas Library)
Dynamic Communicators Workshop
Great Talk Outlines for Youth Ministry
Help! I'm a Junior High Youth Worker!
Help! I'm a Small-Group Leader!
Help! I'm a Sunday School Teacher!
Help! I'm an Urban Youth Worker!
Help! I'm a Volunteer Youth Worker!
Hot Illustrations for Youth Talks
More Hot Illustrations for Youth Talks
Still More Hot Illustrations for Youth Talks
Hot Illustrations for Youth Talks 4
How to Expand Your Youth Ministry
How to Speak to Youth...and Keep Them Awake at the Same Time
Junior High Ministry (Updated & Expanded)
Make 'Em Laugh!
The Ministry of Nurture
Postmodern Youth Ministry
Purpose-DrivenTM Youth Ministry
Purpose-DrivenTM Youth Ministry Training Kit
So That's Why I Keep Doing This!
Teaching the Bible Creatively
A Youth Ministry Crash Course
Youth Ministry Management Tools
The Youth Worker's Handbook to Family Ministry

Academic Resources
Four Views of Youth Ministry & the Church
Starting Right
Youth Ministry That Transforms